Remem Ymar

MW00677107

Wired to Win!

*The Ultimate Guide for Women
Who Want to Plug In,
Power Up,
Push Through to Personal
Greatness*

Sister
to
Sister
Love
Always
Lisa

WIRED TO WIN

The Ultimate Guide for Women Who Want to Plug In,
Power Up, Push Through to Personal Greatness

Copyright@ 2010 by Sharon Frame
Published by Brick By Brick

All rights reserved.
No portion of this publication may be reproduced,
stored in a retrieved system, or transmitted by any
means- electronic, mechanical, photocopying, recording,
or any other- without prior written permission of the
publisher.

To order additional copies of Wired to Win,
or to book Sharon Frame for a dynamic keynote at your
next women's conference, training session, retreat or
special event, call 1 (877) 770-WIRED (9473) or
visit: www.sharonframespeaks.com

ISBN: 978-0-9826780-1-5

Printed and Bound in the United States of America

Dedication

This book is dedicated to my mother, Veleta Jackson. There is no better example of a woman who is "Wired to Win." Ever since I've known her, she has been driven to do better, know more and strive harder to serve others. It's a gift from God that I am forever grateful I inherited. Even in her twilight years my mother continues to plug into purpose and take on new challenges. Ma, you'll always be my Shero!

Contents

A Note from the Author

In the beginning, God created man. And he was good.

But God said, "You know, I can do better."

So He got real creative and made woman. And she was great!

Adam quickly recognized the greatness as she strolled through the garden in all her intoxicating glory.

It stopped him dead in his tracks. His jaw dropped. He stood there spellbound for what seemed like an eternity.

Finally, he hollered out with enraptured delight, "Woh! Man!"

To this day, he's still smitten. But woman oftentimes dismisses her worth or the weight of her ability.

This book is written to remind "Woh-Men" everywhere just how great they are... and how much greater they can become.

We are givers of life. Yet oftentimes we forget to replenish our own.

We delay our date with destiny to support every-body else's dreams. But because we are life-givers, it's never too late to reproduce a better you.

We are pregnant with purpose and possibilities. And like a woman in great labor, we must push to deliver. The better life you are expecting is womb-weary.

It's time. You are well overdue!

Introduction

Born to Win!

My mother had a funny way of losing her eyeglasses. She'd scurry around the house in a frantic search. And just when she had checked every noticeable nook, she'd turn to me in frustration and ask, "have you seen my glasses?" I'd reply with a snicker, "you mean the pair resting above your forehead?"

Imagine hunting for something you already possess. Like my mother, many people are blind to the obvious. They seek purpose and personal success. But few think to look within to find it.

You are a work of wonder. You came to the planet pre-programmed for success. The potential for greatness surges through your veins. In short, you are wired to win! Like a high-tech smart phone, you were designed with so many remarkable features and benefits, it's dizzying. Scientists describe us as an engineering marvel; an architectural masterpiece; a work of pure genius. Each of our more than 50 trillion cells is powered and purposed for greatness. Yet we doubt our ability.

Mind Over Matter

Yes, the body is amazing. But the mind matters more. For "as a man thinks so is he," the Bible says.

So, to tap into your great potential, you must harness the power of your mind.

Here's a news flash: almost anyone can do it. Every day, people just like you defy hardships and difficulties and overcome extraordinary odds to follow their passion. You'll meet a few of them later.

Many have chased their impossible dream until it ran out of breath and finally had to say, "all right already, you win." They use obstacles to fuel their drive to succeed. They have learned to retrain their brain. They have forced their minds to submit to discipline and have fun doing it. So can you. For you too were born wired to win! The journey through these pages will help you plug in, power up and push through to personal greatness.

GET READY TO GET
RE-CHARGED.

Wired to Win!

For those who long to find the secret to success,

Journey within

You'll discover we humans are already wired to win!

At the core of every soul sent to earth to explore

Rests the blueprint to greatness, the itch to do more

Uncovering your full potential is the tough road in life

But walk bold in your destiny, triumph in your strife

For God has empowered you to conquer anything

Just simply believe you are wired to win!

Your desire to climb higher is no wistful yearn

But a cry from your spirit that often goes un-discerned

It beckons you now to embrace the difficult tests

And never to give up trying, never settle for less

Just know that the enemy comes not from without

But is that evil companion, the one called self-doubt

It strips your faith as fear hems you in

And makes you forget you are wired to win

But God took great pains to program you well

And equipped you with talents and skills to excel

So push hard through the difficulty and never give in

You're bound to succeed, for you are wired to win!

—Sharon Frame—

CHAPTER 1
SEIZE THE MOMENT!

CHAPTER 1

Seize the Moment!

Now Is the Time to Plug into Your Dreams

—A Chance Meeting with Time—

I ran into Time today. He was moving with focused and deliberate speed. "Hey, slow down. Wait for me," I yelled. "Take it easy. What's your rush?"

Time shot me a cutting glance and said, "I wait for no man, especially those who squander and abuse me." Then he turned the corner and eased out of sight.

I raced ahead to catch up with Time. But Time just kept marching on. Like an old battle-worn soldier, he moved briskly to the cadence of a familiar drumbeat. Left, right, left right, tick-tock, tick-tock... Time marched on.

But Time's passing insult had wounded me. I demanded an apology, or at the very least, a proper explanation of the charges dropped at my door. When did I ever misuse or waste time, I thought with a huff?

Suddenly, as though he heard my vexed protest, Time stopped in his tracks and doubled back in my direction.

"What right have you to take offense to the truth?" he snapped. "Was I not there when God called you out of eternity--and into me?"

"Did He not fling you in time to fulfill purpose? But here you stand consumed with self-righteous ranker. Is there nothing to show for the Master's investment? Step forward with proof if you have used me well."

Time waited for my reply. But I stood still. His words pierced my heart and shamed me greatly. I cowered in a dark corner along the road, awestruck and speechless. My mind raced back to the many years lived unspent. The talent, the skills, all wasted as I waited for just the right time to "be."

How clearly now I remember Time's earnest urging back then. "Now is the time," he kept pressing. "Now is the time to live your dreams. Step out and walk in destiny. Pull on your faith and fly. You have what it takes to excel to great heights."

Oh yes! I believed! I was convinced. Time was indeed on my side. But in that very moment of personal triumph, Fear slithered in.

"Come now my child," he said, "is all this talk of living your dreams really practical or even realistic? Beside, you've got time. Time to be cautious, be sure, play it safe."

Yes, caution ruled that day, and countless others that followed. So now here I stand, beaten down by a life of "quiet resignation" and empty fulfillment. My dreams are dashed, my hopes long-faded, now running very short on time.

Can I somehow catch up? Perhaps redeem the time? Recapture my dreams? Truly live my purpose? I grappled desperately for an answer.

Time stood still, touched by my woeful state and shameless tears of regret. He looked at my downcast demeanor and said with a deep sigh, "I will pass this way again. But I will not linger. I will not wait. He who is wise will heed the call to greatness. Those privileged enough to get a second chance, must seize this moment in time and run with determined urgency. Destiny awaits you. Now is the time to act!"

"WIRED" RULE #1:
SEIZE THE MOMENT

"Plug In" Points to Ponder

 Time is one of our most precious commodities. It's also one of the most wasted. We are each given 24 hours every day to make the most of each opportunity.

Many people miss destiny because they let time pass. As we grow older, time flies. What dreams have you aborted because you squandered time?

What goals have you put on hold waiting for "the right time?" Now is all you've got. Don't waste another minute. **Get started!**

"Power Up" Quotes

 "Don't wait for extraordinary opportunities. Seize common occasions and make them great. Weak men wait for opportunities. Strong men make them."

—Orison Swett Marden—

"I held a moment in my hand, brilliant as a star, fragile as a flower, a tiny sliver of one hour. I dripped it carelessly, Ah! I didn't know, I held opportunity."

—Hazel Lee—

"You may delay, but time will not."

—Benjamin Franklin—

"Push Through" Challenge

 List five things regarding your heath, wealth or spiritual growth that you have been putting off.

Prioritize your list.

Put a reasonable deadline for each project.

Share your plan with a friend or family member who can hold you accountable.

Treat yourself to a small reward after you have completed the task.

Join my "Wired Up" teleconference. Learn more follow-through strategies that will help you get things done fast.

The Value of Time

Imagine there is a bank that credits your account each morning with $86,400.

It carries over no balance from day to day.

Every evening it deletes whatever part of the balance you failed to use during the day.

What would you do? Draw out every cent, of course!

Each of us has such a bank. Its name is TIME.

Every morning, it credits you with 86,400 seconds.

Every night it writes off, as lost, whatever of this you have failed to invest to good purpose.

It carries over no balance. It allows no overdraft.

Each day it opens a new account for you.

Each night it burns the remains of the day.

If you fail to use the day's deposits, the loss is yours.

*There is no going back. There is no draw-
ing against the "tomorrow."*

You must live in the present on today's deposits.

*Invest it so as to get from it the utmost
in health, happiness and success!*

The clock is running. Make the most of today.

*To realize the value of ONE YEAR, ask
a student who failed a grade.*

*To realize the value of ONE MONTH, ask a
mother who gave birth to a pre-mature baby.*

*To realize the value of ONE WEEK, ask
the editor of a weekly newspaper.*

*To realize the value of ONE DAY, ask a
daily wage laborer with kids to feed.*

*To realize the value of ONE HOUR, ask
the lovers who are waiting to meet.*

*To realize the value of ONE MINUTE,
ask a person who missed the train.*

*To realize the value of ONE SECOND, ask
a person who just avoided an accident.*

*–To realize the value of ONE MILLI-SECOND, ask
the person who won a silver medal in the Olympics.*

*Treasure every moment that you have! And trea-
sure it more because you shared it with someone
special, special enough to spend your time.*

And remember that time waits for no one.

Yesterday is history.

Tomorrow a mystery.

Today is a gift.

That's why it's called the present!

—Author Unknown—

CHAPTER 2

YOU ARE WIRED
TO WIN!

CHAPTER 2

You Are Wired to Win!
So Plan Not to Lose

—Not a Set Back, But a Set Up—

Imagine having your bags packed for three years with nowhere to go. That was me in 1998. I was living a miserable life in a southern city I no longer wanted to call home. My boxes were packed, but I would not budge.

I was too lazy, too scared or too discouraged to give up the familiar. To hear my diary tell it, I was a washed up local TV news anchor in a dead-end job. Things got worse at the TV station where I worked. I soon got demoted. In the television news business that could mean the news director is ready to toss you out like last week's crumpled news paper. Demotion is the pre-pink slip; the first step back before the big push out the door.

Perhaps the boss just wanted a perkier, fresher face. Maybe a new consultant with something to prove didn't like my news delivery. (Or my make-up, my hand gestures, or my dangling earrings.) It was always something.

Once I had to take practically my entire on-air wardrobe into the studio to test the poor lighting on the news set. They were ready to blame the problem on my famously colorful outfits. But for the record, I suspect the general manager simply refused to invest the money it took to fix the lighting problem. But consultants were paid to find fault. And usually, the anchor took the fall.

Maybe the primetime newscast was tanking under my watch. So, I was to be the sacrificial soul thrown on the altar to appease the ratings god.

Whatever the reason, my star power fell faster than a comet hurling through space with deliberate speed. Of course it was a blow to my ego. Certain death to my public image, I thought. What would viewers think? Would my loyal fans see me as a failure?

Worry over public humiliation tortured me. I imagined people whispering snickering remarks as I walked into the grocery store or the beauty salon. Some would flash me the "loser" sign with their thumb and index fingers.

In a crisis, it seems we always imagine the worst or the ridiculous. And we never think we'll recover from a major career setback. Until we do.

Remember, I was miserable before the demotion; stuck in a rut of personal discontent. So fate stepped in. And the push from my highfalutin' anchor chair stunned me. It also forced me to re-assess my personal journey. I began to examine why I had settled for mediocrity along the way.

It occurred to me this setback might not be such a bad thing. I could choose to view it as a set-up to a new chapter in this saga called life. If I was game, I could even see this as an exciting challenge. As I mentioned, I was already packed. So I figured, why not take a leap of faith and just quit my job!

But that meant getting radical and taking some huge risks.

"WIRED" RULE #2:
TAKE CALCULATED RISKS TO DRIVE YOUR SUCCESS

"Plug In" Points to Ponder

Sure, the financial meltdown of 2009 may still have you spooked. Risky and reckless behavior was to blame.

But not every risk is bad. In fact, you can't progress without stepping out and taking a chance. Your success depends on it. The greater the right risk, the greater the reward.

"Power Up" Quotes

"Progress always involves risks. You can't steal second base and keep your foot on first."
—*Frederick B. Wilcox*—

"To win you have to risk loss."
—*Jean-Claude Killy*—

"You'll always miss 100% of the shots you don't take."
—*Wayne Gretzky*—

"Push Through" Challenge

 What big dreams are you pursuing?

What calculated risk have you taken to push your dreams forward?

Write down your goals. Set aside 15 minutes of quiet time every day to read, reflect and reassess them.

Join my "Wired Up" teleconference. Learn fail-proof techniques to break through limiting beliefs.

Chapter 3

Headed the Wrong Way?

CHAPTER 3

Headed the Wrong Way?

Change Direction

—Follow Your Dreams & Think Big—

They say the meaning of madness is repeatedly doing the same thing and expecting a different result. Many people choose the madness because change scares them. But change is the engine that powers personal growth. The alternative is a false sense of security in a "comfort zone" that offers very little comfort.

I'd had enough misery in my comfort zone. So I took a risk that dramatically changed my life. Two weeks before my 10th anniversary at the TV news station, I submitted my resignation. I also put my house on the market for sale. I then determined it was time to pursue a long-held dream, to work for CNN.

The house that Ted Turner built was hailed as "The Most Trusted Name in News." I identified with the daring, bright-eyed maverick. He had a bold vision and believed in the impossible. Ted Turner set out to build the first-ever 24-hour news network.

The cynics laughed. The critics called him crazy. Who in their right mind would want to watch news around the clock? They scoffed at and mocked the young upstart. And CNN was laughingly labeled the "Chicken Noodle Network."

But Ted Turner was wired to win! He simply ignored the naysayers and kept his hand to the task. Their criticisms likely fueled his desire to succeed even more.

Ted Turner's dream not only become reality, it set a world-wide standard and forever changed the coverage of news.

—A Window to the World—

The world likes people who can do things well. It's even more thrilling when they beat impossible odds to succeed. We admire business pioneers like billionaire Bill Gates. He dropped out of Harvard to start a little company you may have heard of called Microsoft--only the largest computer company in the world! Talk about plugging into greatness!

Yes, Gates enjoyed a comfortable upbringing and went to an exclusive prep school. But so did quite a few other people who haven't made a blip on the radar screen of history or philanthropy. Wealth and proper family pedigree can't buy passion. Neither do they equal true success.

The truth is we admire Bill Gates because, with a gazillion dollars in the bank, he's one of the world's richest men. But we admire him more because he plugged into his vision and worked it.

As a young man obsessed with an uncommon dream, he was bold enough to radically shift directions. He dropped out of Harvard University to pursue his passion.

—Against All Odds—

Sarah Breedlove was also bold enough to take a pivotal turn in life. And it led her to greatness. Sarah was a child of the Deep South's harsh depravation. By age seven, she was orphaned when her parents died of yellow fever. By twenty, she was windowed after a lynch mob hung her husband.

But she had a vision to better her life. Sarah found it hard to get good hair products for black women, so she developed her own.

In 1905, she packed up her daughter and moved west with $2 to her name. Just nine years later she was savvy businesswoman and a freshly minted millionaire. Her innovative line of hair care products had exploded, and lured customers from across the country and the West Indies.

History knows this pioneering icon as Madame C.J. Walker, one of the most famous African-American inventors. This daughter of a newly freed slave became the first black millionaire in the country. Determination pushed her out of poverty, prejudice and illiteracy.

She pushed even harder because she knew she was wired for success.

—High Flying Thinker—

My friend Iris Robinson may not have made history like Ted Turner or Madam C.J. Walker.

But she is a big thinker too. We share a passion for travel. She believes the only way to live is first class. Some people might call her over the top. Once, she packed up her delicate china and stemware and flew them from Dallas to Atlanta to throw me birthday brunch.

Then there was the time she hatched a plan to visit Switzerland. Why? To open up a Swiss bank account, for the bragging rights, of course. She showed up at a bank in Zurich with two hundred dollars. One hundred was for her account. The other was start-up money for a promised account for me.

What a shock Iris got when the teller casually informed her she needed a minimum upfront deposit of a quarter million bucks per account! Her stunned look of disbelief almost gave her away. But Iris, she quickly swung her head high, held her composure and said to the teller, "I'll get back with you."

The point is Iris always saw herself as worthy of the very best. She believes thinking big is her birthright. She once visited a luxury car dealership dressed to the hilt. It didn't matter whether or not she could afford anything on the lot. Iris simply wanted to test drive a fine car. It gave her the thrill of feeling worthy to ride in the very best. Iris loves to live large and cares less what people say or think of her.

We have traveled to some of the most beautiful parts of the world. Nothing beats lounging on the exotic beaches of Bora Bora in the South Pacific, or parasailing in Acapulco. Our yearly getaways have expanded our borders and our minds.

You may have dreams that seem an ocean away. I dare you to stretch your mind and imagine that anything is possible. When we give ourselves permission to dream big, ideas and resources gravitate towards us.

My friend Iris plans to be on empty when she leaves this earth. She quips quite often, "When I clock out, I want my tomb stone to read, 'I had a ball!'"

"WIRED" RULE #3: DREAM BIG!

"Plug In" Points to Ponder

Real estate mogul Donald Trump once said, "As long as you're going to be thinking anyway, think big."

Consider this: our subconscious mind cannot tell the difference between an imagined thought and reality. So you become what you choose to think. What you practice, you manifest.

What you routinely conceive, you'll achieve, good or bad; big or small. It's up to you.

"Power Up" Quotes

"Make no small plans for they have no power to stir the soul."

—*Niccolo Machiavelli*—

"Think little goals and expect little achievements. Think big goals and win big success."

—*David J. Schwartz*—

"Give your dreams all you've got and you'll be amazed at
the energy that comes out of you."

—*William James*—

"Push Through" Challenge

What would you love to do if you had un-
limited time, money and talent?

You've got 20 minutes to list 100 things
you'd like to do before you die. Go!

Do something radical this week to step outside your comfort zone. For instance, make reservations at the most
expensive restaurant in town. Go in and order dessert.
Get comfortable, feel worthy.

Join my "Wired Up" teleconference. Learn the art and re-
wards of big thinking.

CHAPTER 4

PROFESS THE POSITIVE

CHAPTER 4

Profess the Positive

—"The World Is Plotting to Do Me Good!"—

Imagine getting up each morning believing every person, every experience you encounter is collaborating on your behalf and in your favor.

It may seem presumptuous to say the world is plotting to do me good. But I will it so.

This philosophy is called inverse paranoia. It sounds rather silly or nonsensical. Before you dismiss it, try it on for size. It might just fit your need to stay positive in perilous times.

It is in the heart of man to dwell on the negative "what ifs." Our fixation with what all could go wrong traps us in life's thickets. Yet we seldom question why we humans have this natural bent. By nature, we readily embrace or expect the worst possible outcome of a seemingly troublesome situation.

Two days after your annual physical, you get an unexpected call from the doctor. You automatically think the worst.

We see "suspicious" movements in the dark and fear we are being followed.

Turns out, it was our own nervous shadow that triggered the fright.

Whether bad or good, we become what we think. This philosophy clearly suggests that much of what we fear is self-inflicted. They are mental musings formed in a person's head. And the longer we nurture these negative notions, the more they grow into natural tendencies.

But the cure for paranoia is also formed in the mind. Just call it positive thinking. We can use it to reverse our fearful thoughts. Use it to foster a philosophy that expects the world to work in concert with us. Indeed, our positive expectations can create powerful, positive outcomes.

Remember, we are the masters of our minds. Too often though, we allow our thoughts to master us. If they are based on fear and negative energy, that's exactly what they'll produce in our lives. If they are powered by positive thoughts, positive results will be our reward.

If we command our minds to follow productive orders, everything within us will follow suit. Even the universe will bow with gladness. It eagerly waits to join your push towards positive purpose. Believe that the world is plotting to do you good. And watch how radically your perspective shifts.

You will not only look at everything differently. You'll get busy and work hard to help make the plot succeed.

"WIRED" RULE #4:
PROFESS THE POSITIVE

"Plug In" Points to Ponder

 In order to develop positive thoughts, we must first get rid of the negative ones. Think of depression, fear and anxiety like drugs that are additive.

So, deliberate intervention is needed to kick the habit.

We attract what we think about. If you find a task too difficult, it may not be. But because your mind thinks it is, it is. The opposite is also true.

The Law of Attraction delivers what you habitually focus on.

"Power Up" Quotes

 "Wherever you go, no matter what the weather, always bring your own sunshine."
—*Anthony J. D'Angelo*—

"The positive thinker sees the invisible, feels the intangible, and achieves the impossible."
—*Author Unknown*—

"A pessimist sees the difficulty in every opportunity; an optimist sees the opportunity in every difficulty."
—*Winston Churchill*—

"Push Through" Challenge

 Identify and document your negative thought pattern.

For one day, carry a pen and note pad. Jot down every negative thought that invades your mind.

When a negative thought hits, say, "cancel" and visualize the opposite thought.

Fix that positive mental image firmly in your mind. Allow only thoughts of empowerment.

Stay away from toxic people. Join the Optimist Club.

You will have what you say. So every day, affirm what you want, no matter how things look.

Join my "Wired Up" teleconference. Learn breakthrough techniques to destroy negative thinking.

CHAPTER 5

DON'T EVER GIVE UP

CHAPTER 5

Don't Ever Give Up

—Shipwrecked—

A couple set sail on the velvet-blue ocean for a lazy weekend get-away at sea. Instead, they got shipwrecked by a sudden and perilous storm. All that surrounded them were miles of lashing waves. Help was nowhere in sight.

The turbulent winds blew fiercely. The couple's frantic hope of getting rescued grew dimmer with every passing day. When food and drinking water ran out, fear and panic set in.

On day 27, the desperate man just couldn't take it anymore. He figured even death was better than the torture at sea. So, he jumped overboard and drowned.

On day 28, search crews spotted the crippled boat and rescued the feverishly weak and half- starved woman.

What a difference a day makes!

Today may be the day you feel shipwrecked at sea. Life's storms seem ready to swallow you up. And as far as the eye can see, there is only a sea of sadness. Help is nowhere on the horizon.

Indeed, life's challenges can overwhelm us at times. And even though we've been tossed and tried before, new setbacks still stun us. We seem all too ready to wonder about our worth or question our ability.

The once-steady plan to pursue a better life falls victim to sudden doubt.

"Could we be off course," we ask, as soon as we hit a bump in the road, or a crashing wave on the high seas.

But now is not the time to consider bailing out. In fact, there is never a good time to give in to the feeling of giving up. No matter how strong the urge to abandon hope, we must cling on for dear life. If you must, struggle with one nostril above water. But don't be swallowed up by the feeling of failure or hopelessness.

Sure, darkness will close in on your bright and happy plans now and then. But don't let it choke the life out of your will to press on. So your compass may be broken, and it seems you're drifting aimlessly. Remember, another day is dawning. Don't be found jumping overboard, just as fate prepares to toss you a lifeline. It's always too early to give up.

Hang on.

You possess the power to persevere through any wretched shipwreck.

"WIRED" RULE #5:
NEVER GIVE UP!

"Plug In" Points to Ponder

 We all experience failures and adversities in life. Some throw us off course. Death, divorce and job loss are just a few of the giant joy-killers.

No matter how devastating the setbacks are, don't take your eyes off your goal. Keep your dream steady in your front-view mirror.

Use setbacks to make you more defiant and determined to fulfill your dreams.

"Power Up" Quotes

 "You always pass failure on the way to success."

—Mickey Rooney—

"A quitter never wins and a winner never quits."

—Napoleon Hill—

"Failure? I have never encountered it. All I ever met were temporary setbacks"

—Dottie Walters—

"Push Through" Challenge

 When was the last time life knocked you down? Go back and examine your response.

So your promising business venture was a flop and a financial sink hole. Move on!

So you fell off the wagon with you weight loss resolution. Try again.

This week, choose one past goal that you failed to accomplish. Tackle it with a vengeance.

Join my "Wired Up" teleconference. Learn strategies from people just like you who turned their shipwrecks into stepping-stones to success.

CHAPTER 6

SEE IT TO BELIEVE IT

CHAPTER 6

See It to Believe It

—A Blind Girl with Clear Vision—

No one would have blamed Helen had she cursed the world and chosen to live a lonely, bitter life.

After all, by some people's measure, she was wretched, with little worth; a girl trapped in a body that refused to work normally. Before Helen turned two, a childhood disease left her blind, deaf and dumb.

Just imagine coming into a world flush with bright and endless possibilities. Yet you are forced to live in utter darkness. Imagine having anxious thoughts racing through your mind. But they can't break through to give voice. And just imagine the birds chirping on a spring morning, and you can't hear them.

Despite her triple handicap, Helen defied the odds to excel. She overcame tremendous obstacles, because even though she was blind, her mind was clear on what she wanted out of life. She wanted to live with meaning and purpose.

—Locked in a Prison Inside Her Head—

No sound, no sight, no real voice. Yet, Helen Keller was born wired to win. Her parents refused to keep her locked in isolation. So they hired tutor Annie Sullivan to help their daughter connect and communicate with the outside world.

The breakthrough came one day, by chance. As Annie poured cool water into Helen's hand to communicate the word "water," her precocious pupil suddenly made a crucial link between the physical flowing liquid and a mental image of water. It was a thrilling, life-changing moment.

The revelation broke open the floodgates and with it, Helen's unquenchable thirst for knowledge. The blind girl had caught a vision and from that point on, she could not be stopped.

She no doubt skipped about the outdoors, touching everything from leaf to bench to bird. She giddily tagged them in her mind with tangible feelings and associations, and tried to mouth out their meanings.

Helen was unstoppable. She mastered Braille and learned to read lips with her fingers. It took her years of grueling practice to learn to speak. Helen was the first deaf-blind person to earn a Bachelor of Arts degree.

She became an acclaimed author and world-renowned public speaker on women's rights.

Here was a blind woman who had vision. She was a deaf woman who heard and heeded the call to achieve greatness.

She was a mute who learned to speak volumes and declared to the world, "Character cannot be developed in ease and quiet. Only through experience of trial and suffering can the soul be strengthened, ambition inspired, and success achieved."

Through the eyes of faith, this blind woman saw herself excelling. She used sheer determination to make it happen. You, who have physical eyes to see, what's holding you back from reaching your dreams?

"WIRED" RULE #6:
SEE IT TO BELIEVE IT

"Plug In" Points to Ponder

Helen Keller had a triple handicap. Yet she excelled. That proves again that will and work are far more important than talent and ability.

The first step to personal greatness is to be able to clearly see what you want out of life. For "if you don't know where you are going, any road will take you there."

More than 130 years after her birth, we are still talking about the famous author and activist, Helen Keller. Are you leaving any footprints behind? What will history say about you?

"Power Up" Quotes

"It is a terrible thing to see and have no vision."

—*Helen Keller*—

"Destiny is not a matter of chance, but of choice. Not something to wish for, but to attain."

—*William Jennings Bryan*—

"The future belongs to those who see possibilities before they become obvious."

— John Scully—

"Push Through" Challenge

 Set time aside to create a vision board. It can help you realize what you want to accomplish.

This is a powerful visual image of your goals. Think of it as your "to-do" list on a poster board.

Pull pictures from your favorite magazines and design the life you want. Dream big and take the limits off your mind.

What will your dream job look like? What exotic vacations would take? What life-saving causes would you support?

Place your vision board in an area you frequent the most.

Examine it every day. You'll achieve your goals faster if you affirm them regularly.

Join my "Wired Up" teleconference. Learn how to create an effective vision board. Discover the power of the subconscious mind to turn images into reality.

CHAPTER 7

BEWARE OF THE GROOVE!

CHAPTER 7

Beware of the Groove!

—A Rebel Just Because—

I have never been much of a conformist. Call me a rebel "just because."

Even as a child, that proclivity got me into some trouble. It seems I was born to defy the status quo.

When it was time to learn to read, I refused. Instead, I figured out a way to memorize the nursery books as my mother or siblings read them to me. As long as they started on page one, I could mouth off the words with delight.

If they turned to the middle of the book, I was lost.

When I got good and ready, I discovered the joys of reading. Now it's one of my most cherished hobbies.

But I still have a rebellious bent, a tendency to go against the groove. What's a groove you ask?

That's the deep gutter people create in the road as they walk aimlessly through life. It is the mindless routine that's become a daily grind. But it's a familiar road most traveled. It's that predictable, safe path people take on their way to an inevitable grave.

It's the road I simply resist.

I rebel against any thought or theory that denies me the right to live a full, balanced, meaningful and wealthy life.

What? Conform to mediocrity when this glorious world overflows with endless possibilities. It dares us not just to dream, but to live the life we have imagined. So, why do so many people get stuck in the groove? It is an unconscious yet debilitating mindset.

Your heart yearns to follow the calling to become an artist. But the groove of reality says that's not a sound career choice. We fall in this groovy reality with little objection, even though what is real is not always true. Remember, we create our reality with our thoughts, good or bad. Since that's truth, why not start developing a new and more positive outlook?

If we don't like something about our lives, we can get out of the groove and change it. But grooves are etched deeply in our brain. They are created by years of habits. These habits occupy our subconscious. They are what forge and form our character. And changing them is most difficult.

That's why well-intended resolutions fizzle so fast. A few days into the New Year, people fall back into the old familiar groove, even though they had so earnestly committed to change.

I have to be a rebel just because that's what it takes to confront the temptation of living in the mundane.

I have to fight against every lazy tendency of be average.

And you too must fight if you want to go against the groove. For it's nothing more than an ever-expanding graveyard. That's where you'll find endless dashed hopes and dreams buried.

I don't intend to reserve a plot. So I'll stay a rebel, just because.

"WIRED" RULE# 7:
TAKE THE ROAD LESS TRAVELED, AVOID THE RUT

"Plug In" Points to Ponder

If you wish to live a life with meaning and purpose, avoid the rut. See where the crowd is headed and go the opposite direction.

A rut is the usual boring, mindless routine. Men and women of unusual character make their own way. They don't follow the pack, they tend to lead.

Watchers watch things happen. Doers make things happen. Which one are you?

Doers blaze new trails, they are not afraid to step out on the ledge of uncertainty.

"Power Up" Quotes

"Two roads diverged in a wood. And I took the one less traveled by

And that has made all the difference."
—*Robert Frost*—

"To thine own self be true."

—William Shakespeare—

"Sow a thought, and you reap an act. Sow an act, and you reap a habit. Sow a habit, and you reap a character. Sow a character, and you reap a destiny."

—Charles Reader—

"Push Through" Challenge

 Commit to reading at least one biography per month of an elite, power figure in the genre of any business.

Implement at least three leadership/business/personal strategies per month from your readings.

Determine the areas in life in which you are a "watcher," a crowd-follower or people-pleaser.

Identify a time when you gave up on a dream because of what "people" said.

Ask yourself "how much do I love me?" Learn to value your conviction. Give yourself permission to say "no" more often.

Join my "Wired Up" teleconference. Learn techniques on how to develop boldness and self-confidence and to celebrate your worth.

CHAPTER 8

EXPECT A FIGHT!

CHAPTER 8

Expect a Fight!

—I Will! I Can! I Must!—

Life showed up yesterday and challenged me to a fight.

Just last month we had it out in the ring. Yet here he was, taunting me again.

"I had you cornered once," he bellowed boastfully. "Next time you hit the mat, there will be no getting up."

I almost didn't survive the beating from that last match. For three straight rounds, Life battered me mercilessly.

I quickly learned a few things: Life wasn't fair, he played dirty and often hit below the belt.

Just before the bell sounded, Life crept up from behind and forced my head in a tight chokehold. "So, you think you can whop me," he whispered in my ear.

Then he slammed me in the corner jam with such force, I saw stars flicker and gasped in horror.

Then Life swung me across the ropes and delivered a cruel body blow.

The first one knocked the wind out of me. I wobbled backwards. Like a drunkard staggering in the street, I struggled to keep my balance. But Life was determined to crush my hopes and dreams. His next blow was like a charging wrecking ball. As his swing made contact, I crumbled onto the mat and whimpered in agony.

Even then, Life would not let up. He kicked me in the gut as I lay there groaning in excruciating pain. He pummeled me with discouragement. And I felt defeat tighten his grip.

The punishing blows were deafening. I could barely hear the rallying cries from the sidelines screaming for me to muster strength, to get up. The faint sound kept getting louder.

Then through my swollen and half-blinded eyes, I saw my Past Victories jump to their feet and yell out, "You can. You will. You must!"

Even louder still, they cheered. "You can. You will. You must!"

But I was so exhausted. Yet that loud and lifting chant gained voice in my head.

"I can, I will, I must win!" Those powerful words surged hope into my limp and tired spirit.

Just moments before, I lay there ready to give up. I was down for the count. It would have been so much easier to call it quits, to just allow Life to win.

But here I was, creeping up, finding my second wind. It whisked over me like a mighty force of determination. "I can, I will, I must."

My purpose for fighting became clear again. And that purpose gave me new strength and boldness to confront Life's challenges.

Other bouts before had left me bloodied and broken. But no matter how weak, I always struggled back and pulled myself up off the mat of despair.

True champions may get knocked down. But they never stay in that low place. So, "I can, I will, I must" take my blows and rebound. For Life is a fight worth engaging. No one gets ahead without getting in the ring. No one grows without the force of friction. It is resistance that strengthens both muscle and mind.

It's only when I choose to give up, that Life's challenges stand a chance at victory. Fight I can, fight I will, fight I must. So Life, bring it on.

And let's get ready to rumble!

WIRED RULE# 8:
EXPECT A FIGHT!

"Plug In" Points to Ponder

Examine this possibility: you might be your own worst enemy. Can you trust yourself to follow through on your personal goals?

Do you fight mediocrity and bad habits? Or do you forfeit and settle for aborted dreams and everyday misery?

Remember, as the saying goes, "Hard work pays off in the future. Laziness pays off now."

Don't let average be your default page. Accomplishments, promotions and achievements come from fighting the tendency to settle for being normal.

Assess your strengths. Ask yourself, "How much am I willing to give up in time and resources to reach my dreams?"

"Power Up" Quotes

"The most important of life's battles is the one we fight daily in the silent chambers of the soul."

—*David McKay*—

"Come to the edge. We might fall. Come to the edge. It's too high! COME TO THE EDGE! And they came and he pushed and they flew."

—*Christopher Logue"*—

"It's not the size of the dog in the fight, it's the size of the fight in the dog."

— *Mark Twain*—

"Push Through" Challenge

 All hell breaks loose the moment you decide to go after your dreams. So develop a mental battle plan.

You win mental warfare by controlling your thoughts, which control your actions.

Pace your efforts as you pursue your dreams. A good fighter knows how to leverage his/her strength and go several rounds.

Find a favorite passage of scripture from the bible and/or inspirational book and read it every day.

Set aside "me" time to meditate and renew your mind.

Join my "Wired Up" teleconference. Learn how to become laser-focused in the battle against mediocrity.

CHAPTER 9

CREATE A
SLIGHT EDGE

CHAPTER 9

Create a Slight Edge

—Make a Seismic Shift—

You may not have felt it, but a monster earthquake that ravaged the South American country of Chile February of 2010 shifted your life too. It registered an 8.8 magnitude.

That's mammoth!

NASA's geophysicists say the massive jolt likely shifted the Earth's axis by about eight centimeters, and shortened our days by 1.26 microseconds. That might not seem like a lot. But in life, every second counts. Over time, they add up to minutes. And like grains of sand in an hourglass, enough minutes make days, which stretch into years.

Now, thanks to that quake in Chile, we are one microsecond shorter on time.

But way before the killer quake struck, we have been selling ourselves short by not registering the seismic shifts in our own lives. Geologically, seismic shifts occur in the Earth's crust and can cause major eruptions above ground.

Practically, seismic shifts are those little changes that make a big difference in our lives. Such shifts can be negative or positive.

Let's examine a case in point. What if you wanted to enjoy a rich, more joyful life? Begin by taking small, simple steps to make it happen. Start by doing a blatantly honest self- assessment. Examine what needs to be fixed in your life. Face the truth about your power-draining habits. Identify the impediments that stand in your way.

With that done, it's time for another shift.

Tackle your issues one at a time. If bad spending habits are the demons keeping you from being wealthy, commit to taking a money management class that offers practical and sustainable results. The third shift is to earnestly stick with your plan of action until you conquer that weakness.

I call this the FTC approach. Face. Tackle. Conquer.

Shift One: Face the problem.
Shift Two: Tackle the problem.
Shift Three: Conquer the problem.

This results in positive seismic shifts. Enough of these small steps will yield monumental changes.

Doing nothing also causes a shift. Like the earthquake in Chile, you may not have felt the tremor. But it happened. You may not see how taking -no- action hurts your chance at a better, more fulfilling life. But it does.

Like it or not, what we do every day creates seismic shifts. They eventually trigger eruptions.

For some, personal success will erupt. Others will just shift further into a life of self-defeat.

WIRED RULE# 9:
CREATE A SLIGHT EDGE

"Plug In" Points to Ponder

 The little changes in life make a big difference. It may take you five or ten years to get your college degree. But every small step moves your closer the big graduation day.

Don't despise your small beginnings. Start where you are with what you have. Don't wait for everything to be "just right" to start a new venture. Conditions will never be "just right."

The small steps you take today towards your goal will create the momentum for big results tomorrow.

Don't get discourage if everyone seems to be racing ahead on the road towards destiny. Remember the turtle and the hare.

"Power Up" Quotes

"How do you eat an elephant? One bite at a time."
— *Author Unknown*—

"Steady and slow wins the race."
—*Aesop*—

"Perseverance is the hard work you do after you get tired of doing the hard work you already did."
—*Newt Gingrich*—

"Push Through" Challenge

Commit to making one seismic shift this week. For instance, increase your productivity in small, bite-sized steps. Every day, write three things on a note card that you must accomplish that day.

Do the hardest chore first. Vow not to go to bed until they are done. See how quickly your small accomplishments add up to big personal successes.

Always running late for work? Get a plan in place to shift your habit. Make a daily effort to show up early. Do that long enough, and you may impress the boss. This conscious move may lead to a raise or promotion.

Read Malcolm Gladwell's book, The Tipping Point: How Little Things Can Make a Big Difference.

This week, send someone a small card or simple gift for no special reason. See how it creates abundant gratitude from the recipient and huge joy for you.

Join my "Wired Up" teleconference. Learn techniques on how to double your creativity and fast track your plan for personal improvement.

CHAPTER 10
THE MIGHT OF MENTORS

CHAPTER 10

The Might of Mentors

—You Can't Go It Alone—

Madam reader, I told you earlier how I quit my good-paying job as a local TV anchor. It was a huge calculated risk to pursue my dream to work at CNN. But the thought of working for the first Cable News Network was not mine entirely. That seed was planted by a precocious minister at my church in Hartford, Connecticut.

Elder Eddie Howard had a way of stirring your soul with his fiery sermons. He was determined to snatch every sinner from the jaws of hell. He seemed equally driven to shepherd young Christians onto the right professional path.

From the pulpit, other ministers emphasized being a good Christian. Elder Howard stressed being an effective Christian by walking in purpose, on purpose.

He realized my talent as a young public speaker, and believed in my greatness before I had the courage to do so. One of his favorite practices was to corner me after church for a private counsel. He had a kind and jovial spirit that quickly disarmed any objections. He'd fix his focus. And with a look of faith and firm conviction, he'd say, "Sharon, one day, you are going to work for CNN. You are going to be great. You are going to be the next Jessica Savitch."

At the time, the highly popular NBC network news anchor was the fastest rising national star in the business. Comparing me to such a news celebrity thrilled me. Knowing that someone believed in me and expected me, even dared me, to succeed meant even more.

His faith in me was like fresh morning dew. It nourished self-confidence and gave me roots and reason to think big.

Another mentor was my mother.

—Fighting the Odds—

This is how you know you are goofing off in high school: when your mother brings home better grades than you do, even while she works two steady jobs. No one is more "Wired To Win" than my mother, Veleta Jackson. She came to America from our native island of Jamaica in 1969.

Like many people who migrate to this great land of opportunity, my mother came hungry for a better life. As a young girl, her stepfather had forced her to drop out of school and work the fields. So she had little formal education. She yearned to learn. But that desire had to wait.

Now in America, she quickly set a firm focus on working a menial job to support her five children back in Jamaica. Every extra dime was saved to prepare for our U.S. arrival four years later.

That happened on a brisk spring day on April 3rd. I was an anxious 11 year old. I remember the chill that nipped me as we stepped off the plane at Bradley International Airport.

And there was my mother waiting. Her face was flush with concern and her arms filled with coats for each of us. She handed me what resembled a Little Red Riding Hood cape. I still remember how it snuggled me with warm and wonderful feelings about my new country. And like Little Red Riding Hood, I had no idea what adventures awaited me.

Her children were now safely with her. And not long after we enrolled in school, my mother began to pursue her high school diploma.

Imagine working two, sometimes three jobs, while raising five children. Then, squeeze in time for her schoolwork. But she was "bound and determined" to better her life.

Author Napoleon Hill said "if you can conceive it and believe it, you can achieve it." That might as well be my mother's motto in life. It didn't matter how hard or heavy her burden. Once she made up her mind to achieve something, it would be done.

Not only did she struggle several years to graduate from high school, she graduated with honors. She even pulled better grades in some subjects than I did. Then she went on to start college.

You think "Brutus" was ambitious? That William Shakespeare character could not hold a candle to my mother. And unlike him, her motives were pure.

She wanted to be an example to her five children. One of her most famous household quotes was "nothing beats a failure but a trial (an attempt)."

She expected her kids to try and succeed. She became one of my greatest teachers by the way she pursued her dreams with gusto.

—It's Never Too Late to Dream—

My mother was always fond of music. She tried to pass on that love to us kids by buying a piano, even paying for lessons. But living vicariously through her children would not satisfy her longing. So, years later, she decided to invest in her passion, and hired a piano teacher.

After years of grueling practice, her banging noise finally took on the sound of music. At age 70 plus, she now plays the organ at her church. Her dream deferred would not be a dream denied.

If that was not enough, her passion for helping others has taken deep root in the rich soils of Jamaica. Several years ago, my mother took on a solo task to build a church in her childhood district. Now, you must know she is not a pastor or a minister. She is simply a layperson who saw a need and was willing to sacrifice to make a difference.

It's taken her more than three years. It was taxing and costly. But neighborhood children now have a place for Sunday School and after school activities. And the adults have a place of worship to call their own.

This project has given my mother great joy and a renewed sense of purpose. I draw strength from her unselfish efforts. She has set a pattern that leaves me no excuse for failure. The tenacity and determination I now possess are mere reflections of hers.

Yes, to my benefit, I have inherited many of my mother's persistent qualities. I believe in fighting against the odds. I am convinced failures are mere stepping stones to greatness. They simply reveal what doesn't work.

All we have to do is make the corrections and move on.

—Turn On the Light—

It took Thomas Edison quite a while to get the invention of the electric light bulb just right. When asked about his years of research and setbacks, the great scientist said, "I have not failed. I just found 10,000 ways that won't work."

It was also Edison who defined genius as "one percent inspiration, and ninety-nine percent perspiration."

So, how must sweat equity have you invested in your dreams lately?

"WIRED" RULE #10:
SECURE GOOD MENTORS

"Plug In" Points to Ponder

 I have learned the power of mentors. They hold me accountable. They cheer me on. They dare me to stretch.

When pursuing your dreams, don't go it alone. Seek mentors who are at the level you want to be.

Remember, "Iron sharpens iron." If you are the smartest person in your circle of friends, you need new friends.

Good mentors will make sure you are investing "sweat equity" in your dreams.

"Power Up" Quotes

 "A mentor is someone who allows you to see the hope inside yourself."
　　　　　　　—Oprah Winfrey—

"Mentoring is a brain to pick, an ear to listen, and a push in the right direction."
　　　　　　　—John Crosby—

"No man is an island."

—Thomas Merton—

"Push Through" Challenge

Find a solid mentor to hold you accountable.

Analyze your group of friends and associates. Do they celebrate your dreams or discourage you?

List five powerful people you want to meet. Invite them out to lunch and pick their brains.

Join local women's business groups like the ABWA.

Offer your volunteer services to an organization of which you wish to be a part.

Join my "Wired Up" teleconference. Learn the hidden secrets and power of a mastermind group. Discover the power of leveraging relationships.

CHAPTER 11

LEARN TO PUSH THE ENVELOPE

CHAPTER 11

Learn to Push the Envelope

—Courting CNN—

My father-figure mentor had assured me I'd work for CNN. So firm was his conviction, he had me thoroughly convinced. Not even the passing of two decades could halt my resolve.

So 20 years after his prophetic words, I found myself standing outside the CNN headquarters in Atlanta. It was the summer of 2000. I stood out front gazing at the mammoth red CNN sign on a sweltering hot day. Here is where tourists from all around the world came to prop, pose and snap pictures.

For a split second, I got nervous. And the thought hit me, "Here is where my dream of working for the network could die."

I had flown to Atlanta on a wing and a prayer. For I am not one to live by the conventional rules. I was told to send my resume to the proper CNN department head and wait to hear back. I tend to push the envelope, and "go beyond the common acceptable boundaries."

Sometimes in life, you can't wait to hear back. That call might never come. Use the proactive approach. Create your own way in when there is none. The truth is there is always a way. But we can't see it because we are blinded by fear or timidity.

My CNN job hunting efforts had been fruitless by phone. So, I decided to take a trip and talk my way into somebody's office. The only inside contact I had secured before arriving was not in the news division. But I had convinced this department manager to at least meet with me. Perhaps she was impressed that I'd fly all the way to Atlanta with no guarantees, and so had pity on me.

And there she was with a friendly smile and outstretched hand of greeting. She ushered me into her small office. We talked about niceties for a while. Then she mentioned a position in her department was vacant. It was not a "news" job. She felt I was overqualified and said quite nonchalantly, "I am not even going to offer it to you."

I was miffed but held my tongue. Such an offer she felt would insult me. I saw it as a possible blessing in disguise. Again, all I needed was a crack. Once in, I felt certain I could create a way to get to CNN's news division. But there she was, taking my one shot off the table.

Another setback, another failed attempt. But I kept hearing elder Howard's voice drumming like a cadence in my head: "One day you are going to work for CNN."

With that reminder, I pressed the kind lady for suggestions or any contact she could share. That's when she mentioned the man who would later become my boss. But even with that, it was to be an uphill battle. After an interview and a writing test, I headed back home empty-handed.

But I was undaunted.

Sure, I had no job. And life looked bleak. For a minute, I nervously wondered if I was wise or plain dumb to quit my job before I found another. But it's been my observation that when I leave myself no other choice, I tend to kick into high gear and accelerate my efforts. Call it motivation or call it desperation.

Whichever it was, I decided to move to Atlanta anyway, and be closer to the fight. I pushed the envelope and got the call to start as a freelance news writer. Soon, I was anchoring for HLN, formerly CNN Headline News. For a while, I also anchored for CNN Airport News and CNN Student News. I also wrote for CNN Domestic, as well as CNN International.

The belief in a long-held dream paid off through dogged persistence.

Elder Howard died before I made my CNN debut. But I'm convinced he was seated in his La-Z-Boy recliner in Heaven, glued to the tube, daring anyone to change the channel. That day, he was my biggest fan.

Several years later, I dreamed I met my dear mentor outside my home while on a visit to Connecticut. I had just stepped out of a car when he walked up to greet me. I was giddy with excitement. "Elder Howard," I hollered. "I made it! I made it on CNN!" He flashed that lovable, Cheshire cat grin and nodded as if to say, 'I know!"

—Oprah's Calling!—

I was out in the field covering a story when I got the call from the assignment desk. My boss wanted to talk to me. The last time I got an urgent call to a boss's office it was not good. Then, I was working at a TV news station in Raleigh, North Carolina. My photographer and I got into a nasty argument. As I recall, we were not seeing eye-to-eye on our assignment. That was nothing new. This photographer was a brilliant guy. But it seemed he always wanted to do just enough work to get by. The details are sketchy. I must have challenged him and he took offense. He then got on the news car's two-way transmission system and started airing our dirty laundry. Everyone in the newsroom could hear his tantrum.

Not to be outdone, I followed his lead. Sadly, I was not walking in patience, love or long-suffering that day. I fired off my self-defense with an animated tongue-lashing. Like two spoiled brats, we hurled accusations until we got back to the station.

The "closed-door" meeting with the boss was not pretty. In my mind, I should have won the argument. Instead, I got the lion share of the reprimand. I never figured out why. One thing was very clear though. That day, I lost a personal battle over self-control. Lesson learned.

But that was a different time, a different station. Now, word of a meeting with the boss was peppered with excitement.

Producers with the Oprah Winfrey Show had called! They had stumbled across a bizarre local story I had covered, and were smitten.

It had to do with a young man who was mistakenly pronounced dead by the parish coroner. He had been missing for a while. Then a body washed up on the Red River. The young man's family set a date for his funeral, made arrangements and bought a coffin.

Just days before the service, his mother answered a ring at her front door and was almost paralyzed by shock. There stood her "dead" son, alive and well.

It appears sloppy work in the coroner's office led to a botched ID match of the missing and the dead. The coroner had a lot of explaining to do.

Oprah wanted this juicy story. My job was to follow the family to Chicago, capture their experience on the show and report it.

But what peaked my excitement was the chance to meet and interview the long- reigning queen of day-time talk. I had already envisioned the encounter and considered the probing questions to ask. But a feisty show producer abruptly dismissed that idea. She told me on the phone in no uncertain terms, Oprah was going to be too busy after her show to talk to me.

"Excuse me? No way am I flying up to Chicago and not get a one-on-one interview with Oprah," was my reply.

Now, most reporters would have accepted being told that Oprah's schedule was jam-packed that week. But I pressed the issue, and asked nicely to speak to another producer. I got nowhere.

Even when I arrived in Chicago, I was told there would be no time for an interview. To make matters worse, I was informed the show was overbooked. That meant I had to watch the taping not in the studio, but from the sideline! Over my dead body!

Tell me, how often do you get a chance to meet the woman who would become "the world's most powerful woman?"

Thomas Edison once said, "Many of life's failures are people who did not realize how close they were to success when they gave up." Well, I was not about to give up on this once-in-a-life time opportunity.

So, I pressed, argued and cajoled until a senior producer caved in. But she informed me Oprah only had five minutes to spare. Not a problem, that's all I needed. What I got was twenty-five minutes with Oprah, who was most gracious. The five-part special series I squeezed out of that interview still ranks as one of my most memorable experiences in the broadcasting business.

Oh yeah, I also knocked out my original assignment: a pretty good story on the "dead" guy's family dilemma and their big day on national TV with Oprah.

Are you allowing life to "assign" you destiny? You'll fall short of your potential.

You take control. You push the envelope on your goals. And don't let small minds lock you into their limited mindset.

"WIRED" RULE# 11: SOMETIMES YOU HAVE TO PUSH THE ENVELOPE

"Plug In" Points to Ponder

Sometimes success comes only after we press beyond acceptable boundaries.

Your dreams are too important to take "no" for any answer.

If it's to be, it's up to me!

"Power Up" Quotes

"When the world says, "Give up," Hope whispers, "Try it one more time."
    —*Author Unknown*—

"Consider the postage stamp: its usefulness consists in the ability to stick to one thing till it gets there."
    —*Josh Billings*—

"There is no telling how many miles you will have to run while chasing a dream."
    —*Author Unknown*—

"Push Through" Challenge

 Call up your cable provider or you car insurance agent and ask for a better rate. Argue your point courteously. Feel the surge of power that comes with being bold and confident. Even if they say no, you'll feel ten feet taller.

If you are shy, join Toastmasters International and sign up to deliver a speech a month later. Volunteer to speak extemporaneously during club meetings.

Read Susan Jeffers' book, Feel the Fear and Do It Anyway.

Join my "Wired Up" teleconference. Learn the secrets of conquering the enemy called fear and the power of laughter.

CHAPTER 12

FOLLOW THROUGH. FINISH STRONG!

CHAPTER 12

Follow Through. Finish Strong!

—Fight to the Finish—

Have you ever had to face the naked truth about yourself and instead ran from the mirror? Some time ago, I noticed a recurring habit stood in the way of me moving from "good to great," from mediocre to mighty.

It was a nagging habit of inconsistency. Having prided myself on being a person of plan and purpose, it took me a while to admit I had this problem. But the evidence was mounting.

So, just how many projects had I started and failed to follow through on? I did a little self-inventory and was brutally honest with me. It was disturbing.

Confession: I am a big picture person who easily gets bored by cumbersome details. So, a current task is sometimes left in my wake, as I am swept up by another "fun" project.

You see, once the thrill is gone, I tend to leave right with it. What was left was a lot of unfinished business waiting for me the next day. This was a character flaw I had to address. And I discovered it had a history.

I remember being such a smart 4th grader I was bumped to the 6th grade. But I quickly realized 6th grade work was tough. I made a few good faith efforts, but gave up.

I simply refused to buckle down and embrace a consistent study habit. Instead, I packed up my books and marched myself back to 5th grade.

A year later, 6th grade was right there waiting for me, along with that same taskmaster of a teacher I didn't care for.

Then, there was the time I joined Toastmasters International. What should have taken perhaps a year to complete the first battery of speeches, took more than five. I had a bad habit of periodically "dropping out" of the club to pursue, what else, more alluring adventures.

Since this habit was deeply entrenched in my make-up, I had to fight vigorously to root it out. Had

I not, this periodic nuisance would have become a dangerous pariah.

When we don't follow through, crucial matters are left undone. That slows progress. Inconsistency keeps us frazzled, off focus and out of control. You feel like there's a hole in your soul that needs patching. But it only gets stitched up.

Inconsistent behavior leaves us unprepared, running late, and filled with excuses. This often results in missed opportunities.

One too many of those can derail destiny and destroy a shot at living a glorious, more rewarding and purpose-driven life.

So, the big fight is to follow through. Complete a task. Stay steady at the helm once you set a course. You won't enjoy all the work involved. The thrill may vanish at the first feeling of discouragement or boredom.

But it's perseverance that gets the job done. It is what separates the great from the good, and winners from losers.

I intend to squeeze every drop of value out of life. And my past inconsistent habit has robbed me of too many chances to fill my cup. Not anymore.

No more being drained of focus and fulfillment.
Too much is at stake.

*So, the battle is on to follow
through and finish strong!*

"WIRED" RULE #12:
FOLLOW THROUGH,
FINISH STRONG!

"Plug In" Points to Ponder

 Let me be quite candid, I have not arrived. But I am wired to win. And every day I take seismic steps towards greatness. The fantastic challenge for any of us is to finish strong.

Because we are pre-wired for success, even with our issues and character flaws, we can accomplish just about anything we put our minds to.

So don't sweat the periodic set-backs or failures. They only remind us we are made of sterner stuff.

Don't get discouraged if your dreams and hopes seem dashed. You just focus! And follow through.

"Power Up" Quotes

 "When you get right down to the root of the meaning of the word "succeed," you find that it simply means to follow through."

—F. W. Nichol—

117

"Those who are blessed with the most talent don't necessarily outperform everyone else. It's the people with follow-through who excel."

—*Mary Kay Ash*—

"It was character that got us out of bed, commitment that moved us into action, and discipline that enabled us to follow through."

—*Zig Ziglar* —

"Push Through" Challenge

 Take one suggestion from each chapter of this book. Commit to incorporating them in your life and follow-through.

Get a "follow-through" journal to document your actions. Set aside time once a week to review them.

Purchase and watch the movie "Rudy." It chronicles the inspirational story of Daniel "Rudy" Ruettiger. His real-life tale of an unlikely University of Notre Dame football player is persistence personified.

Join my "Wired Up" teleconference. Learn winning strategies that push you to higher levels of emotional, professional and spiritual growth.

Push!

....

Like a woman in great labor

Yearning to deliver

I too am fully expecting

Growing deep within me

Is this great self vision I see

Content no more to be

Just fair to middling

Conception was oh so sweet

The ecstasy full and complete

As this seed of desire

Was planted in my womb

I fantasized, idealized

Of all I could become

Weighted down in pregnancy

A burden of expectancy

To live life with greater satisfaction

Push!

To realize my deepest dreams

To leave some footprints on the scene

And be sure to count

And make some sort of difference

But no one ever warned me

It's in labor and delivery

Where dreams can surely die

When hard work is not applied

So, like a woman in great labor

Straining to deliver

I too must push with fervor

Push beyond discomfort

Push beyond the pain

Push beyond the agony

Lose all dignity and shame

For my dream has too much import

To just grow weary, then abort

Or in the end, bear stillborn

This hankering for a better me

So, like that woman in great labor

Fighting to deliver

Facing wrenching pain

While on the very brink of death

I too must push to gain

Push against that lame tendency

To be average or exist just normally

And settle for an insipid life

Half-full or worse, half-empty

So, despite miscarriages of the past

I now must put my hands to the task

And push,

Until I feel that final thrust at last

And hear that sound of victory

That yelping cry of delivery

A burst of new life and energy

Which proves I -can- produce

A more marvelous me!

—Sharon Frame—

RULES TO

Plug In,

Power Up,

Push Through

to Personal Greatness

"Wired" Rule #1
Seize the Moment

"Wired" Rule #2
Take Calculated Risks to Drive Your Success

"Wired" Rule #3
Dream Big!

"Wired" Rule #4
Profess the Positive

"Wired" Rule #5
Never Give Up!

"Wired" Rule #6
See It to Believe It

"Wired" Rule #7
Take the Road Less Traveled, Avoid the Rut

"Wired" Rule #8
Expect a Fight!

"Wired" Rule #9
Create a Slight Edge

"Wired" Rule #10
Secure Good Mentors

"Wired" Rule #11
Push the Envelope

"Wired" Rule #12
Follow Through, Finish Strong!

Join my "Wired Up" teleconference. Get life-changing strategies that will position you to follow your dreams, get more of what you deserve and live your best life now!

Plug in to www.sharonframespeaks.com to stay powered up and motivated. Break through limiting beliefs. Get unstuck. Learn to take fast action through my personal one-on-one coaching.

About the Author:

Sharon Frame is a former CNN anchor, awarding-winning journalist, public speaker and personal empowerment coach.

Her mission is to encourage, inspire and empower the willing to live their most fulfilling, productive life.

Her primary focus is women who are hungry for personal and spiritual growth.

She has spent more than 20 years as a local television anchor/reporter.

She has conducted countless power-packed keynotes and seminars on personal and career achievement.

Sharon Frame also the author of The 67th Book of The Bible. This compelling spiritual journal has been translated into French. It is the basis of a life-changing 12-month biblical home/church study course.

She lives in Atlanta, Georgia.

Book Sharon Frame to give your next meeting or conference a dynamic, positive power surge.

*Learn how at www.sharonframespeaks.
com or call 1 (877) 770-WIRED (9473)*

Follow her "Wired to Win" blog at www.sharon-framespeaks.blogspot.com

CPSIA information can be obtained at www.ICGtesting.com
Printed in the USA
BVOW041945200512

290602BV00001B/1/P